Cupid's

Secret

Writing Irresistible Personal Ads

How to write personal ads using the powerful marketing techniques of professional ad agencies including over 500 super-charged words, phrases and examples to inspire you

by Mark Petterson

www.EasyReaderPress.com

Harness The Power of Professional Writers

Ever been reading a magazine or watching TV and some commercial ad really grabbed your attention? Well, that commercial was scripted by a highly paid writer known in the trade as a copywriter. Copywriters don't just fall out of trees, and it takes years and years of practice plus large amounts of talent to write the kind of commercial ad that grabs attention.

Writing a personal ad is no different.

But the good news is that the same tried and true techniques that go into crafting a powerful and compelling commercial ad can work just as well for you. Even better, 99.9% of online posters have absolutely no clue how to do this.

Which guarantees you the competitive edge in the crowded world of online dating.

So maybe you're not getting enough responses to your online dating profile. Or worse, you're getting too many of the wrong kind of responses. Or maybe you're just starting out and want to really stand out from the ocean of mediocrity.

If so then it's time to turbocharge your profile by exploiting the same powerful marketing techniques ad agencies use. The basics are simple and easy to use once you know them. Even better, I'll walk you step-by-step through the process from A to Z. And along the way I'll give you over 500 compelling words, phrases and other examples to help spark your creativity or even use for yourself.

By way of introduction I've been a professional writer for thirty years. By 'professional' I mean I earn good money from my skills. I've worked for ad agencies, magazines, corporate marketing departments, politicians, and private individuals – all looking for that crucially-important competitive edge.

My book will give you that edge.

Here's just some of what I'll cover:

Choosing a fun and unique user name

Using subliminal suggestions in your profile pictures

Knowing what to bait your hook with

Nine headline types that get you noticed fast

Starting your profile with a bang for maximum impact

Your profile narrative – what to include, what not to include, and how much to include

Emotional triggers – 63 key words that arouse emotions

Advanced psychological techniques

Building your profile toward a powerful close

The call to action – motivating others to get in touch with you promptly

The importance of reinventing yourself and how to do it

Losing losers

Rejecting rejection .

And over 500 super-charged examples to kickstart your creativity

So are you ready to find someone special? Then let's jump right in.

TABLE OF CONTENTS

Introduction

Now that everybody and their pet monkey have signed up with online dating services you'd think it would be easy to hook up with someone neat. But for various reasons it's just not so simple. For one thing you're awash in an ocean of mediocrity and you've got to stand head and shoulders above the crowd. For another, you need to deliver your message to the right people so they'll respond back.

Ad agencies have made a science out of successfully marketing products, and these very same techniques can work for you.

Maybe it seems a bit tawdry, marketing yourself like some product, but don't think of it that way. You're unique and special, you possess an abundance of life-energy, and you're searching for a wonderful new relationship with someone as special and unique as you are.

So let's get started.

It's All About Marketing

First off, you need to understand that your personal ad is a 'sales tool'. Sorry if that sounds a little impersonal but it's true. And if you think about it most of life is about sales: talking yourself out of a speeding ticket, convincing someone to hire you, persuading your boss to give you a raise, and most importantly – finding someone wonderful to share a relationship with.

Ad agency writers understand that successful marketing is all about demand creation. While you're not a new car or box of cereal writing a power-packed online personal ad is really all about marketing you in such a way as to generate qualified responses.

Sure, you're bound to attract some losers, but the trick is to generate enough targeted quantity that a high degree of quality is mixed in.

That way you can pick and choose who to respond to.

Creating Demand

OK, so just how do you go about creating demand and selling yourself?

Imagine walking onto a car lot and the salesperson rushes up and yells: "My kid needs braces, my wife wants new shoes and I need a big commission so buy this car!"

Hmmm, were you convinced to part with your hard-earned money? Of course not.

But what if that same salesperson said: "Picture yourself in that cool convertible cruising down the back roads with the top down. It goes from zero to sixty in seven seconds, gets terrific gas mileage, and comes with free oil changes."

Do you see what that salesperson just did? He tried selling that car on all the wonderful benefits it would bring to you.

So now you know the first and most important key in successful sales: sell yourself on the benefits you'll bring to a relationship.

Three Key Questions

In order to successfully market something a professional ad agency writer must first answer three important questions:

1) *What is the product?* That's you, of course, but you're a pretty complex person, aren't you? Which means boiling you down to just a few paragraphs will be difficult. But don't worry, I'll show you some tips and techniques later on.

2) Next, *who is your audience?* In other words, who do you want to respond? Some cute twenty-something who's all about next weekend's rave? Someone more mature who'd rather visit a museum than a heavy-metal concert? Or maybe a mellow retiree with no kids and plenty of free time? The better you know who you're looking for the better you can craft your message.

3) The last question to ask is *what is the purpose of your ad?* What is it that you want to find? A friend? A casual relationship? A long-term partnership?

You may wish to go into greater detail here about the individual characteristics of your ideal match. How important is religion to you? Politics? Personal habits? Intelligence? And so forth.

Call this your criteria list. It's for your eyes only and not for your public profile.

But the true value of this criteria list is helping you decide quickly who to reject and who to respond to.

So take a moment to answer these questions right now. The more focused you are the better.

A Fun Assignment

Now here's something fun to do: check out your competition. Why? Because you want to get a feel for what you're up against. Make a note of what you like and don't like. See anyone you know? Hee hee, sometimes it's amusing to see what they think of themselves.

Basically, we're stirring the pot here, getting your creative juices flowing.

Choosing a User Name

You need an online name, of course. Hopefully it will be great, but simple works, too. Your initials with one or more numbers is fine. Or play around with an activity you like.

When you surfed the competition did you see any screen names you liked? Try changing them around a bit to make them your own.

But have some fun with it. You might try making a list of places and things you like. Say your first name is Ian and you like Hawaii. Put 'em together for HawaiianIan. Maybe you know your way around sailboats. ReefKnot or HalfHitch might do. I ride motorcycles so my first user name was ElectraGlideMark.

However, stay away from anything overly cute or suggestive or negative. What does Candypanties say about that person? Or CaveMan? You get the idea.

Now here's a very easy way to brainstorm a name: do an Internet search using the keywords 'name generator' or 'nickname generator'. You'll find several sites that will create a unique name for you, some better than others. How does Introverted Extrovert sound? LiberalConservative? HobbitSniffer? StumpToe? Well, mileage varies but with enough effort you'll find something distinctively you.

Your Picture

I'm absolutely astounded by how many people put so little effort into their picture. I mean, really, would you take a vacation without seeing some great pictures of your destination? How about opening a book without a great cover? People are visual and like attaching a face to who they're reading about. Give it to them. At least five pictures but go the limit if you're so inclined. However, follow these guidelines.

Do not stand in front of a mirror and snap your own photo. Are you so dull and uninteresting that's the best you can do? Of course not. But when you researched your competition I bet you saw a lot of that, didn't you?

Do not use a previous picture of you and your ex cut in half. Hey, I can see that arm around your shoulder and it's a turn off.

Do not hire a professional photographer to stage a glamour shot. Yes, you will look absolutely fabulous. But if you don't look that way on a casual lunch don't do it. Unless you're a movie star. And if you're a movie star that's just so sad that you're here reading this. But for the rest of us, the point of your posted pictures is to give the viewer a chance to see the real you.

Use recent photos, of course.

Quick story: I have a close friend who's witty, charming, smart and good looking. But she's handicapped and uses a wheelchair. After six months of getting a good online response she admitted to me that most of them bailed when they learned she was handicapped. I suggested including at least one photo of her in the wheelchair. She gets less responses now but the ones who do email are serious.

Later on I'll show you the profile I worked up for her.

The Necessary Photos

Get a good head shot of you looking your everyday best. Smile. Look right into the camera with those beautiful eyes of yours. You'll need a friend to help with this, or a digital camera with a timer. Take the picture outside during the day with the sun behind the camera. Snap several photos so you can pick the best. But pick just one.

Next, snap a photo of you doing something active and interesting. Make the photo close enough to clearly see your face from another angle. One of my photos shows me raising a pair of binoculars to look at something in the woods. A bird? A bear? A nudist camp? Doesn't matter. But it shows I do interesting things and have a life.

You could be hoisting a boat's sail, or pruning a rose bush, or frosting a cake, or starting a camp fire. The purpose here is to make you seem visually interesting. So what do you like to do? I hope it's not munching chips and watching TV all day.

Now take another action shot, but be looking in the opposite direction from the above shot. And be doing something interesting, too, but different. I know you enjoy life, so this is how you let the viewer know. Of course these photos are posed, but if you're not looking into the camera and are doing something interesting no one will notice. Make sure your lovely face is clearly visible in each of these shots, too.

And you don't have to smile in every photo, either.

One of the purposes of these photos is to show you involved in activities you like, activities that you'd like to share with others. These types of pictures carry powerful subliminal messages and help weed out people who aren't interested in bungee jumping or tightrope walking or whatever else you enjoy doing.

To round out your photos mix in some friends. You're a likeable person, right? One of my photos shows me at my writers meeting sitting at a table full of other writers all scribbling on pads. Maybe I'm writing the next great American novel. Maybe I'm writing a dirty limerick. Doesn't matter. I have a social life. Another of my photos depicts me on my Harley at a Christmas Toy Run. Shows what a caring guy I am, with a little bit of adventure mixed in.

Note that with all my photos, and especially with the last two, I'm pre-qualifying who I want to respond. If you haven't read a book since dropping out of grade school pass me by. If you think only hairy outlaw thugs ride motorcycles then go back to your knitting club.

So the ultimate use of your photos is twofold: to attract responses from people who like your looks and share your interests, and to pre-qualify who responds. If your passions are cultivating exotic roses and collecting Hummel figurines you're probably not looking for NASCAR fans or circus acrobats. But who's to say that might not work out?

Now here's what you probably shouldn't have in your photos, and I'll explain why. No pictures of you and your darling kids. I'm sure you're a great parent but let me discover that later. Same with shots of you and dear old Granddad, or your sweet and precious labradoodle, or anything else that doesn't create demand.

Remember that we're selling you on the benefits of getting to know you. How does your grandma benefit the reader? Or your precious pig-eyed pugapoo? Same with beautiful sunsets unless you're in the picture. And so forth.

If your profile photos don't somehow sell you as interesting and popular and fun and adventurous – or whatever else you really are – then save those photos for an album. That's why you figured out who your audience is earlier. That's who you're marketing yourself to with your pictures. It's all about sales, baby.

Now, it is OK to have a few shots of you so far away that your face isn't immediately recognizable, but you'd better be doing something interesting – like parasailing over the Grand Canyon, or swinging upside down on a trapeze, or flossing a live alligator.

I'm kidding, of course, but keep in mind when you're far away you look like a stick figure. So be doing something your target audience is interested in, and don't mix in other stick figures because how will we know which one is you?

Now on to the eight most important words in your profile: your headline.

OK, maybe I'm exaggerating about the importance of these words, but not by much. Because studies have shown that the very most effective headlines are usually eight words or less. But don't worry, some rules can be bent and I'll show you when and how.

The Headline – Nine Types Geared for Results

(Not all sites utilize headlines, of course. In which case you'll use the headline as the first line in your narrative. Either way, the whole purpose is to create reader interest.)

Aside from your profile picture, the first impression someone gets about you is your headline. And you want such a great headline that the reader is compelled to read further.

So what do you bait your hook with? Simple – a reason. Give the reader a reason for continuing. And since you know your audience you'll understand those reasons.

Now, a great headline does four things: draws attention, selects the audience, delivers a message, and then pulls the reader into your narrative.

But first, let me show you types of headlines to avoid: *Where are you? Where is my true love? Why haven't you found me yet? Where is my prince charming? Where is my queen?*

The common factor in the preceding examples is they're all about what the writer is looking for. But see, right now the reader is doing the looking and your job is to get the reader interested in you and what you have to offer.

Remember the car salesman? The headline is where you start selling yourself on the benefits of getting to know you further.

So how do you write a great headline? Here are the nine best headline types with examples. (I've included many more great examples at the end of this eBook).

1) The **direct headline**

> *Country Boy On The Hunt*

> *Nerdy, Sexy, Cool*

> *Lioness In Search of Her Simba*

2) Next is the **indirect headline**. This is a little more subtle, using curiosity to raise a question in the reader's mind which will be answered in the narrative.

> *Not all blondes love diamonds*
>
> *5 Secrets no one knows about me*
>
> *Why you shouldn't read any further*

3) The **news headline** is self-explanatory.

> *Fresh On The Market!*
>
> *Introducing A New Adventure!*
>
> *Guaranteed Non-fattening!*

4) Now here's the **how to headline**:

> *How to skin a cat the right way*
>
> *How not to write an online profile*
>
> *How I can make you smile*

5) Next is the **question headline**, one of my favorites.

So why do I like it so much? Because the right question attracts a viewer's attention and causes them to wonder what the answer is. And that is the first step in involving the viewer in you and your profile. Since you already know who your audience is you'll be able to pose exactly the type of question that will interest them.

Now, there are two ways to pose this question. One is short and simple, yet it sets the tone for the very next sentence. And remember, the whole purpose of the headline is to get the viewer to read the next sentence in your profile. And the next sentence after that. And so on.

When you read the following examples imagine how you might answer them in your own profile:

> *Ever Walked A Mountain Trail In Spring?*

> *Do The Neighbors Call The Cops On You?*

> *Does Spooning Lead to Forking?*

This is a short, simple and effective approach. For it to work best it must involve something actually about you, addressed to your audience. Notice that most of the questions contain or imply the word 'you'. The last sample uses humor. Be careful with humor, though, not everyone has a sense of humor. We'll go into further detail on how to follow up your short question later.

So what if you want a headline longer than eight words? No problem. We'll call this type the *split headline*.

Just be sure to keep it engaging. With a longer headline you put the first several words in the headline and then finish it up in the first sentence of your profile. Many of the following partial headlines are finished up in the back of this book so you can see how it goes, but if you read one and feel inspired see what you can come up with.

6) The **split headline (question)**

> *Is it just me, or...*

> *Have you ever laughed so hard that...*

Tell the truth, wouldn't you rather...

The **split headline (statement)**

There I was, minding my own business when...

I promised my goldfish that...

I get all the news I need from...

7) The **cool quote headline**

There's an old saying in my field: Good writers imitate, great writers steal. So why reinvent the wheel if someone else already said something great?

I've included some samples here, but the very best way to find a great quote is to search the internet. Pick just about any subject that's close to you – love, sports, the beach, boating, friendship, traveling, thunderstorms – whatever, and there's probably a great quote about it. And remember that if it has meaning for both you and someone else, well, you've already found something you both share in common. (many more examples are included in the back of this eBook).

Don't put the key to your happiness in...

The more I get to know some people...

Dear drama, I'm breaking up with you...

Now here are some cool love quotes you can try out:

You can't put a price on love, but...

If love is blind why...

Love is a fire. But whether it will…

Now here are some catchy company slogans:

It's your world, take control

Dreams made real

Discover what's possible

If you find it difficult brainstorming your own catchy phrase then the Internet is just a click away. These particular search parameters will help stoke your imagination: 'Catchy phrase' 'Short quote' 'Romantic quote'' Best Motto' 'Best business motto' 'Best slogan' 'Memorable movie line'.

8) Next up is the **command headline**:

Read this now

Jump into life

Escape the mundane

9) Finally, we have the **testimonial headline**. Copywriters love this one because it presents outside proof that you offer great value.

Nine out of ten doctors recommend…

Experts agree that…

Voted most fun because…

What Comes Next – The Lead Paragraph

Your lead paragraph should directly relate to your headline by answering the question or otherwise satisfying your reader's curiosity. It should also start introducing you in such a way that the reader wants to read the next paragraph.

It's better to have loved and lost than…

…to do forty pounds of laundry a week. Plus running a household, raising three kids, two dogs and the occasional hamster, and keeping it all within a strict budget. I wouldn't trade those memories for anything but now it's time for making new memories.

93% of all serious snow skiers believe that…

…Jackson Hole is the very best place for catching big air or bombing. Not that I do much of either, but I do enjoy a long day carving through the powder followed by an evening of hot chocolate in front of a roaring fire.

The day I broke up with normal…

…I had a fling with insanity. Didn't work out too well so now I'm normal with a twist.

Now if any of the previous samples apply to your own life by all means use and personalize them. If not, reflect on something you did that was fun or memorable or scary or whatever.

But here's the key: Don't say you like to hike, write about the gold and black butterfly you saw flitting among the pines. Don't say you like to watch comedies, describe the teenager in the next row who laughed so hard he snorked his soda. Do you like cold snowy nights? Then describe the aroma of logs burning in your fireplace as the wind drives snowflakes past your window. Are you a gardener? Help me smell the roses and hear the buzzing bees. Do you like sailing? Let me hear the crack of the sail when you come about.

What we're doing here is painting a picture in the reader's mind that involves as many senses as possible – sounds and aromas and sights and touch and taste and so forth.

The key with your headline is making the viewer want more. The key with your first paragraph is to introduce yourself in a unique way and reveal something about you. Are you humorous? Philosophical? Intellectual? Romantic? Nerdy? Put it out there because that's the audience you want reading your profile.

The Narrative

So now that you've created an exceptional, memorable, unique and personalized headline followed by a compelling first paragraph, let's move on to the main narrative.

The good news here is that if someone has read this far then you're definitely on the right track. They're interested. So let's keep them interested.

Basically, a good profile consists of three parts: beginning, middle, and end. Your headline is actually the beginning of the beginning, and since you came up with a great headline it won't be hard to make the opening line or paragraph relate to it.

So what should you put into the next few paragraphs following the first paragraph?

The Narrative: Middle

The middle is more about you and some about who you're looking for.

You can't put everything here so concentrate on a few significant brushstrokes. Keep it simple, interesting and relevant and you'll do fine.

Remember that even as you're writing about yourself you're still marketing. And what is marketing all about? Demand creation - selling yourself on the benefits of knowing you.

Here are some traps to avoid:

Negativity. Do you like being around negative people? No, and no one else does, either. Sure, you've probably had your heart bruised but now is not the time to complain that most men are bums, or that you've had your fill of greedy little gold-diggers.

Never. Not. Nothing. No. Try and avoid these words.

I'm always amazed when I read someone's profile that says: *'No games!'* or *'Scammers Stay Away!'* or *'Serious Replies Only!'* Do people really believe that will stop anyone? If that really worked banks could simply put up signs reading: *'No robbers allowed!'*

The next trap involves mentioning how much your children, pets, family and/or friends mean to you. I'm sure they all mean a great deal to you and that's a good thing. But when I read something like that I wonder how far back in line I'll be in this relationship. Your children, pets, family and friends are not really selling points to me.

Another trap is mentioning how hard you work and that you hardly have any time left over. I get it, but where will I fit in with your schedule?

Lastly, if your significant other passed away, or you're in the middle of a terrible divorce, then I am so very sorry, but please don't share it in your profile. Most of us are here for new beginnings and new chapters in our lives. Allow yourself all the time you need to grieve and heal, otherwise you risk either turning other people off, or worse, attracting some sort of scum-sucking predator.

Words That Arouse Emotions

Now, men and women approach and read personal ads in different ways. We don't need to get into the science here, so let's focus on something simpler – keywords. Scholarly research has shown that certain words evoke emotional responses in women, while other words evoke emotional responses in men. These words are called 'emotional indicators' and this subject was first written about in 1965 by W.P. Brown and published in the *British Journal of Psychology*.

So if you really are interested in the science behind it all start with that publication.

Words That Appeal To Women (26)

Here are some words that trigger positive emotional responses in women:

affectionate

animal lover

animated

clever

confident

dependable

flexible

family-oriented

fine-dining

happy

inspiring

interesting

intriguing

invigorating

joyful

kind-hearted

loyal

passionate

polite

respectful

romantic

self-assured

sincere

talented

travel

witty

Words Or Phrases That Bore Women (20)

Now here are a number of words or phrases to be cautious using:

active

clubs

energetic

fun guy

great sense of humor

I don't know why I'm doing this

ladies

live life to the fullest

movies

nice guy

outdoors

outgoing

sexy

shy

single

sports

the water

what's up

working out

What Men Like About Women

Research shows that men generally like these traits in women: confidence, a sense of humor, altruism, being genuine, not appearing needy, spontaneity, being passionate about something, able to bring out the best in their partners, femininity, physical fitness, emotional fitness, optimism, playfulness, intelligence, peaceful, supportive, fun, health conscious, affectionate.

Words Or Phrases Men Like To See (20)

Here are some keywords that men like to see in a profile:

adventurous

big heart

chemistry

classy

culture

down to earth

educated

fun

girl next door

graduate degree

intelligent

masters degree

sexy

small town

smart

sophisticated

spontaneous

versatile

vivacious

witty

Turn-Off Words Or Phrases For Men (22)

If you're a woman looking for a man try and keep these words or phrases out of your profile:

Ballet

Candlelit dinners

Commitment

Decrepit parents

Friends first

Hate sports

Love cats (or worse that you own several)

Marriage

Meaningful relationship

Mother or Mom

Must have own car (or teeth, or job)

My friends / children convinced me to do this

No games!

No losers!

Normal

Opera

Raise pit bulls

Rainbows

Soulmate

Sunsets

Symphony

Walks on the beach

Next, avoid clichés like the plague. And stay away from overused phrases like this:

Not into games

Serious replies only

I'm no good at these things

I've never done this before so here goes

Think Out Of The Box

Now, I know you're a pretty versatile person with lots of interests and activities but try and stay away from phrases like *I am just as comfortable at a black-tie affair as I am wearing jeans at a backyard barbeque.* Yes, it's easy to write and covers a lot of ground but everyone says something along those lines. Think out of the box. Show, don't tell. *After I spilled chili on my best tux (long story) I decided to use it for camping clothes. You should see the looks I get from Park Rangers.* I bet you got a good visual from that in your mind. But what was inferred in those two lines are that I own and use a tux, that I'm human enough to spill chili on myself, that I like camping, and that I have a sense of humor.

Remember that your profile should be just a few major brushstrokes. If you give away everything what will you talk about over lunch?

Whatever you eventually decide to put into your profile narrative keep in mind that I'm reading your profile because I might like getting to know you better. So if I do try to get to know you what's in it for me? I already know what's in it for you, which is me, and I'm a pretty good catch. So keep your middle upbeat and interesting, but don't get too wordy. Lead them on but leave them wanting more.

The Close

Lastly we come to the close. Sales professionals sometimes term it 'The Call for Action'. In other words you're asking for the sale. Or in this case you want a response. Be short. Be specific. And don't leave any doubt about what you want the reader to do next.

Here are a few examples (more in the back!):

Interested? Shoot me a line.

Let me know if you felt a spark.

Email me and let's see what happens.

And One More Thing...

Consider using a P.S.

In sales letters, studies show that after reading the headline many readers scan down to the end of the letter to read the P.S. next. Whether that holds true for an online profile nobody knows yet, but adding a P.S. to your profile is both unique and attention-grabbing. It can also serve to reemphasize a selling point or to add in a time factor as a final call to action.

P.S. I just discovered a great new Thai restaurant. Let me tell you about it!

P.S. Guess what new fantasy novel my 12-year old daughter can't put down. Ask me the title!

P.S. If you love coffee there's a new specialty dark roast out just for the holidays. Want to know where to find it?

P.S. Spring is finally here! How does enjoying a glass of wine at the Sidewalk Bistro sound?

Stay Loose

As you write your profile don't stress out on the wording. Stay loose, stay comfortable, pretend you're talking to a good friend. The best writing sounds like conversation.

You know not to use ALL CAPS. And please pay attention to spelling and grammar.

Truth to tell professional writers go through several draft versions of the final product. It's called polishing your work and it never hurts. So when you're done put your work away for a couple days, then look at it with fresh eyes.

Let some friends read it and get their opinion. One of the gals in my writing group brought in her profile for us to work on. We did such a good job that within five minutes of posting the new version she received 200 offers of marriage, a seven-figure book and movie deal, an athletic gear sponsorship, a life-time subscription to Popcorn of the Month Club, and complementary use of a corporate jet.

I kid you not.

Stay Fresh

Every so often many retail stores move their displays and merchandise around. This makes everything look new and fresh, and people often see items of interest they missed on their previous visit.

You should do this, too.

A good rule of thumb is to change your main picture, headline and profile every three months. People who viewed you once may take another look. People who passed over your first profile may like your second version better.

Yes, it involves more effort, but that's why you took a bunch of pictures to begin with, right? And that's why you're reading this eBook, for inspiration and ideas.

You'll also get a better idea of what works best for your targeted audience. I once wrote a profile that I thought was screamingly hilarious. Apparently I was the only one who thought so. The only response I got back was from someone who thought it was so bizarre she was including it in her book of all the losers she met online. I'm offering it as one of my examples in the back of this eBook, but you've been warned. Oh, and if anyone comes across her book of online losers drop me a line – I'd like to know who my competition is!

Advanced Psy-Ops

Now we come to what truly separates the amateur writer from the real pro – an understanding of some very advanced theories and practices. This is how the very best copywriters can sell you on something without you even realizing you've been sold to. Here's how they do it:

The first step is strategically analyzing your readers' emotions and psychological triggers. Then craft your words with subtlety. Easy reading is hard writing, and expertly written copy is an intricately planned strategy. Each word is included for a reason, including how it is used, where it is placed, how it sounds, what it means, the punctuation around it, the length of the word, the length of the sentence, the length of the paragraph, how the word relates to the word six lines above it and the word six lines after it.

Complicated stuff, I know. But this is what really good copywriters know how to do, and why the very best get paid so well.

Show, Don't Tell

The key is to draw readers into the moment. How? With vivid images and details.

Visual is good. But your eyes make up only 20% of your senses. Try mixing in sounds, smells, tastes, and touch. And don't forget tactile elements such as temperature, texture, and pressure (a hard rain or a soft caress, for instance).

Sell the Sizzle

There's an old maxim in copywriting that you don't sell the steak, you sell the sizzle. In other words you're selling the experience. Read any vacation brochure or watch any ad – whether it's about clothing or perfume or food – and you'll see they're all about selling the experience.

The Harley-Davidson Motor Company is a master of this. Go to their website and check out the pictures. Each one has a bike in it, but the setting is always someplace you immediately want to visit, on a Harley, of course. They're selling a lifestyle, not transportation. Now check out their apparel catalog and the descriptions. I just went to my closet and counted eleven motorcycle jackets and leather vests. Man, those Harley writers are good!

And it's exactly the same with you – you're not really marketing yourself, you're marketing yourself as a great experience.

Bottom line your words are all about manipulating the reader. With the right sensory images you can influence the reader's emotional and mental state. You can excite them, relax them, make them happy, make them sad, but hopefully make them want to find out more about you. Demand creation, in other words.

White Space

You need it. So no long paragraphs. Why? Because readers like text presented to them in bite-sized, easily-digestible pieces. Otherwise, they're reminded of some boring and dull textbook they were forced to read by some boring and dull teacher.

It's OK to have lots to say, but it's not OK to say it all in one paragraph.

Entertain

People like to be entertained. Some people are entertained by the Discovery Channel while others get their entertainment from the Comedy Channel. But since you already know your audience you know what pulls their trigger.

By 'entertain' I don't mean tap dancing while humming the Stones' greatest hits on a kazoo. But tell a story. Reveal something. Be interesting. Engage curiosity. Build drama. Or whatever appeals to your core audience. The key is to keep your reader's interest levels up.

Iconicity

Now here's a big word to impress the rubes with: *Iconicity*. Basically all it means is that sounds have meaning. You might also call it *phonetic legerdemain* if you need some more big words.

We're into hyper-advanced graduate-level copywriting here, so no falling asleep in class.

Digging deeper, iconicity actually means that the characteristics of certain words (the sounds) symbolize certain meanings and communicate these feelings and emotions to the person hearing or reading them.

Sign language is an easy example for understanding iconistics because sign words usually have a more direct connection to the idea or object they're symbolizing. The sign word for *you* is simply pointing at the person. The sign for *cry* is putting your index fingers under your eyes and drawing them down.

A great many spoken words also carry symbolism but are often more subtle.

Take the letter j, for instance. It's used to start several aggressive words such as jab, jerk, jam, jinx, and so forth.

The s sound can suggest motion: swirl, sooth, swell, swivel, sail, sulk, smooth, swing, slide, slither and so forth.

Generally, the larger an object the more likely it will have open vowel sounds in its name. Open vowel sounds can also be associated with round shapes and dark or gloomy moods – moon, doom, moan, groan, balloon. The smaller an object is the more likely it will have a closed vowel sound. Closed vowel sounds are sometimes associated with pointed shapes and happy moods – scrap, hat, cat, pet, wit, pup.

Enough Already, How Do I Use This Stuff?

If you want an edgy feel use *z, q,* or *k*.

For a feeling of serenity use flowing sounds.

To impart energy use sharp vowel sounds. A softer feeling is achieved with softer vowel sounds.

Syntactic Iconicity

You've got to be kidding, there's more? Sure, entire college classes are taught on this stuff. But unlike my last professor, I'll be brief.

Syntactic iconicity is just a fancy way to define word order and rhythm. It's what poets do really well. And it makes for nice reading in your profile.

Keep your sentences short and to the point. But once in a while mix it up with a longer sentence, or even a sentence fragment. Limit the length of your paragraphs. A one-sentence paragraph adds variety. Ask a quick question. Then answer it. Blend serious with witty.

But above all try and have fun with your profile. 'Cause you're a fun person, right? And everyone likes to be around fun people.

Losing Losers

The first reader to review my book penalized me one star for not including some surefire way to keep losers from responding.

Believe me I wish I knew that secret.

Because the truth is we all get losers, liars, scammers and suckwads contacting us. It's a numbers game to them – pester enough people enough times and sooner or later someone will be naïve enough to respond.

You won't be that person, of course, because you've already installed 'filters' into your personal ad

The first filter is your pictures. As already discussed they reveal certain truths about you: your age, your looks, what you play at and so forth. That will screen out some of the people that aren't a good match.

So if you're fifty-something and some twenty-something contacts you step back and take a deep breath. Sure, it's very flattering, but c'mon, what are they really after?

And if you're twenty-something and some old fossil writes you, well guess what? Same deal.

Remember that some of your pictures should show you engaged in your favorite activities. Not only does this help attract people of similar interests, but it also provides a great way for another person to get a conversation started. Which is exactly what you want.

However, if someone contacts you and says something totally irrelevant or really dumb regarding your pictures then *BOOM* – hit the delete button.

The same goes for your profile. As you recall the whole purpose of your narrative is to engage someone's curiosity and give them valid reasons to reach out. So if someone contacts you and doesn't in some way reference either your pictures or your narrative then *POW* – hit the delete button.

So now you have two great filters to help weed out the losers.

Here are some additional filters that I use successfully:

Can they write a complete sentence? Can they spell? Do they use a bunch of totally irritating emoticons?

Even worse for me is when someone sprinkles in chat acronyms or text abbreviations. When they do I just shoot back the message: 2BZ4UQT!

And the last time someone contacted me USING ALL CAPS I hit the delete button so hard it sprained my wrist.

Your filters may differ, of course, but the point is to figure out what they are and then use them ruthlessly. Just don't sprain your wrist.

So while I don't know any guaranteed way to prevent every loser from ever contacting you I can certainly help you avoid the worst of them.

Rejecting Rejection

Let me briefly touch upon a subject that affects us all at some point in time: rejection.

I've been there and so have you.

Doesn't matter if you're online or just living life, rejection is part of our existence.

They key is to keep it in perspective.

How? Here are two good ways:

1) Accept the fact that there are many people out there who are just not looking for you. It's OK.

2) Always remember that you are unique, wonderful, special and strong. You know that's true, don't you? So don't let someone else's opinion of whether you're a good match for them or not bring you down.

It's a very big world out there. And chances are excellent that your special someone is out there waiting.

TA DA!

So there you have it – the very most important secrets to writing compelling personal ads using the selling techniques of professional ad agencies.

And I bet you'll see better results once you put these techniques to work. And deservedly so.

What follows are a bunch of examples you can use, abuse or be inspired by. I know you'll brainstorm something as exceptional and unique as you are.

Examples to Inspire You

Direct Headlines (120)

Here are a bunch of headlines for you. When you read them imagine how you might use them to write the first paragraph of your narrative. Later on I'll show you what I did with some of them.

My bucket list

Funny, creative, smart, handsome, and modest

Will work for cuddles

Swag is for boys, class is for men

Cooking! Food! Art! Music!

Placing a call for commitment

So we'll tell everyone we met at Starbucks

Regular funny guy, inquire within

Blah blah blah

Looking for future soccer mom

Guaranteed more fun than your last filling

Let's help Cupid out

Beautiful bike - hot chick included

The fun aunt

Looking for like-minded hooligan

Cynical optimist

Tired of talking to my dog

New adventures needed

Partner to share senior moments with

Ignore the dumb username

Life is not for spectators

Country boy on the hunt

Nerdy, Sexy, Cool

Lioness in search of her Simba

Adorkable

Teacher by day, uncommon playwright by night

Father, Businessman, Poet

Sometimes keeping it simple is hard

Nerdy but naughty

Bored Diva looking for Pavarotti

Metro-male and modern urban anthropologist

Action hero needs to save someone

When the world zigs, zag

No turning back now

Low mileage and a sense of humor

Stop everything!

Imagineer at work

More fun than your Ex!

Player wants playmate

Outgoing introvert

Witty headline? I got nothin'

When I find you I'll know

Just a simple, complicated girl

If you were a dinosaur

I'll bring the bikini you bring the boat

Mediocre ukulele player

Opporknockity only tunes once

Enough tears, life awaits you

Cooler than the flip side of your pillow

Boy next door with a twist

Error #5498: user too good to be true

Looking for long term relationship

Life isn't complicated, people are

Never too late to live happily ever after

Tall, dork and handsome

I open doors, it's who I am

Curious elegance

Amazing seeks amazing

It's a blessing and a curse being awesome

Awesome knows awesome

Outgoing, outspoken, outrageous

Omnia vanitas (all is vanity)

Big smile, open heart

Beautiful disaster

Easy for you to say!

Tattoos, metal, punk rock

Part ninja, part artist

Laid back nerd

I heart smart guys

As real as it gets

Gotta love tatts

55 is the new 35

Attractive, intelligent, fun

More wag, less bark

You had me at log in

Live, love, laugh, eat, repeat

Multi-faceted Aries seeks new adventures

Nosce te ipsum (know thyself)

YOU! Yes YOU! The one reading this!

Your coach awaits, m'lady

Searching heart seeks new oasis

Good heart seeking same

Jewel of the Nile searching for her Pharaoh

Nubian Princess desires prince

Let me spoil you rotten

I have the key to your heart

I speak fluent Romance

Love is a language best spoken by two

Let's connect the dots together

I know ten ways to make you happy

Never settle for less than you're worth

Experience the sublime

Broken hearts mended here

Searching for new beginning

Gentle man seeks gentle woman

You've found your missing puzzle piece

Open mind, open heart

Namaste

Perfectly imperfect

Imperfect me seeking imperfect you

Sesquipedalian pedagogue seeks polysyllabic etymologist

Chicks in chairs make good roll models

I'm not yelling – I'm Italian!

There is no future in the past

I can be ready in 15 minutes

And here we are again

What's meant to be will find a way

Looking to settle down, not just settle

Slightly wacky is the new normal

Tired of having coffee alone

If the world didn't suck we'd fall off

Rule 85: No excuses!

Be yourself. Everyone else is already taken

I come with a free thirty day trial

Laughter is food for the soul. I'm hungry

I thought you'd never get here

Proud to be awesome since 1978

Mildly crazy seeks same

You can never get ahead by looking back

Indirect Headlines (3)

Not all blondes love diamonds

5 Secrets no one knows about me

Why you shouldn't read any further

News Headlines (11)

Fresh On The Market!

Introducing A New Adventure!

Guaranteed Non-fattening!

5 Adventures You Won't Want to Miss!

Won't Last Long!

Limited Supply!

Recommended by four out of five doctors

Sometimes myths are real

It's not bragging if it's true

The facts of life are wrong

Guaranteed more fun than your last filling

How To Headlines (5)

How to skin a cat the right way

How not to write an online profile

How I can make you smile

How to set your toes on fire

How to mend a broken heart

Question Headlines (27)

Ever Walked A Mountain Trail In Spring?

Do vegetarians eat animal crackers?

Do The Neighbors Call The Cops On You?

Still searching?

Is Your Cat Planning To Kill You?

What's the matter with me?

What do you want to be when you grow up?

What's wrong with this headline?

What Are Your Plans This Weekend?

My Boat Is Sinking. Can You Help?

Why do I need a headline?

If not now, when?

Does Spooning Lead To Forking?

Where do you go to collect smiles?

So what's in this for you?

Why wait until someday when I'm here now?

Wassss up????

Haven't you wasted enough time yet?

Knock, knock. Who's there?

Is it bragging if it's true?

Are the facts of life wrong?

Ever walked the beach in fall?

Cat got your tongue?

What Are Your Plans This Weekend?

What are your favorite passport stamps?

I want the fairy tale. Do you?

I'm here! Now what's your other wish?

Split Headlines - Question (9)

When you read these split headlines imagine how you might complete the next few lines. Of course you can always skip further along and see how I completed some of them.

What do you want to be...
...when you grow up?

Forgive me but...

What would happen if 300 angels decided...

Have you ever laughed so hard that...

How much do polar bears weigh?...
...enough to break the ice so tell me your name.

If size doesn't matter why...
...are they searching for bigfoot and not smallfoot?

Tell the truth, wouldn't you rather...

Is it just me, or...

Instead of sleeping in this weekend, wouldn't you...

Split Headlines – Statement (19)

Top ways I spend my time...

My headstone will read...

There I was, minding my own business when...

I promised my goldfish that...

I get all the news I need from...

They say everyday is a gift but...

The best advice I ever got was...

The dishes can wait, but right now...

Close your eyes and make a wish...
...did you see me?

Let's write a story together where...
...we live happily ever after.

Boy, am I tired of running...
...through your mind all day.

Fluent in sarcasm...
...but it wasn't a language option.

If I had a rose for every time I...
...thought of you I'd be picking roses forever.

Whenever I feel sad I stop and...

...try feeling awesome instead.

Two promises...
...my emails will never be boring and I will never wink.

No one likes to talk...
...about themselves, so I asked my friends.

If you are a queen looking for a...
... king I am that man.

I'm a special kind of twisted...
...So don't try to figure me out.

Reach for the stars...
...even if you only reach the moon you've still gone a long way.

Cool Quote Headlines (38)

Your heart is free, have the courage...
... to follow it. (Braveheart)

I would rather have had one breath...
... of her hair, one kiss from her mouth, one touch of her hand,
than eternity. (City of Angels)

It seems right now that all I've ever...
... done in my life is making my way here to you. (The Bridges of
Madison County)

Medicine, law, business, engineering, these are noble...
... pursuits and necessary to sustain life. But poetry, beauty,
romance, love, these are what we stay alive for. (Dead Poets
Society).

The best love is the kind that awakens…
… the soul, that makes us reach for more, that plants the fire in our hearts and brings peace to our minds. That's what I hope to give you forever. (The Notebook)

Do you ever put your arms out and just…
… spin and spin and spin? Well, that's what love is like. Everything inside of you tells you to stop before you fall, but you just keep going. (Practical Magic)

Destiny is something we've invented because…
… we can't stand the fact that everything that happens is accidental. (Sleepless in Seattle)

I always thought that there was this…
… one perfect person for everybody in the world, you know, and when you found that person the rest of the world kind of magically faded away, and, you know, the two of you would just be inside this kind of protective bubble, but there is no bubble, I mean if there is you have to make it, I just think life is more than a series of moments, you know, we can make choices, and we can choose to protect the people we love, and that's what makes us who we are and those are the real memories. (Forces of Nature)

I'm scared of walking out of this room…
… and never feeling the rest of my whole life the way I feel when I'm with you. (Dirty Dancing)

The day I broke up with normal…
…was the first day of my magical life. (source unknown)

Jump off a cliff and…
…build your wings on the way down. (Ray Bradbury)

Don't put the key to your happiness in…

...someone else's pocket. (source unknown)

He who laughs... lasts! (Mary Pettibone Poole)

All smiles, no regrets. (source unknown)

Listen carefully...
...sometimes opportunity knocks softly. (source unknown)

Those who wish to sing will always...
... find a song (Swedish proverb)

The best advice I ever got was...
...how people treat you is their karma, how you react is yours.
(Wayne Dyer)

No turning back now. (source unknown)

No borders, no constraints. (source unknown)

Always listen to your heart...
...it is on the left but usually right. (source unknown)

The more I get to know some people...
... the more I like dogs. (variation on Mark Twain)

Dear drama, I'm breaking up with you. (source unknown)

I'm not a one in a million...
...kind of girl, I'm a once in a lifetime kind of woman. (source unknown)

Nobody is perfect until...
...you fall in love with them. (source unknown)

Wait for me somewhere between reality and...

...all we've ever dreamed of. (source unknown)

I love people who make me laugh even...
...when I don't want to smile. (source unknown)

Call me old fashioned but I actually take...
...relationships seriously. (source unknown)

Some people come into your life just to...
...teach you how to let go. (source unknown)

Grant me the senility to forgive or forget...
...the people I don't like, the good fortune to run into the people I
do like, and the eyesight to tell the difference. (source unknown)

Forget Monday, get lost in the moment. (source unknown)

The greatest thing in life is finding...
...someone who knows all your flaws, mistakes and weaknesses
and still finds you absolutely amazing. (source unknown)

Sometimes the only blessing you need...
...is to count your heartbeats. (source unknown)

Growing old can be fun if...
...you do it with the right people. (source unknown)

Life isn't complicated, people are. (source unknown)

It's never too late to live happily ever after. (source unknown)

Sometimes I pretend to be normal but...
...it gets boring so I go back to being me. (source unknown)

Oh, you hate your job?...

...Why didn't you say so? There's a support group for that -- it's called EVERYBODY and they meet at the bar. (Drew Carey)

Life should not be a journey to...
...the grave with the intention of arriving safely in a pretty and well preserved body, but rather to skid in broadside in a cloud of smoke, thoroughly used up, totally worn out, and loudly proclaiming "Wow! What a Ride!" (Hunter S. Thompson)

Love Quote Headlines (31)

You can't put a price on love, but...
...you can on all its accessories. (Melanie Clark)

Love at first sight is still possible but...
...it pays to take a second look. (source unknown)

Love is always full time, never part time...
...never sometimes, and certainly never just on your time. (source unknown)

It's not hard to find someone who...
...tells you they love you, it's hard to find someone who actually means it. (source unknown)

One day someone will walk into your life....
...and make you realize why it never worked out with anyone else. (source unknown)

Honesty is the key to a relationship but...
...if you can fake that you're in. (Richard Jeni)

You have to walk carefully in love...

...the running across fields into your lover's arms can only come later when you're sure they won't laugh if you trip. (Jonathan Carroll)

All you need is love, but...
...a little chocolate now and then doesn't hurt. (Charles M. Schulz)

Marriage lets you annoy one special person...
...for the rest of your life. (source unknown)

The four most important words in any relationship...
... are I'll do the dishes. (source unknown)

One good thing about internet dating is...
...you're guaranteed to click with whoever you meet. (source unknown)

Love can sometimes be magic, but magic...
...can sometimes be just an illusion. (Javan)

Friendship is like wetting your pants...
... everyone can see it but only you can truly feel its warmth. (Jack Handey)

When your girlfriend has Taylor Swift lyrics...
...as her Facebook status, you're either doing something very wrong, or very, very right. (source unknown)

If love is blind why...
...is lingerie so popular? (source unknown)

Love is a fire. But whether it will...
...warm your hearth or burn down your house you can never tell. (Joan Crawford)

Love is like Pi...
...natural, irrational and very important. (Lisa Hoffman)

Love is like a password...
...hard to figure out but you always want to keep trying. (source unknown)

Happiness is the china shop, love is...
...the bull. (H. L. Mencken)

Never let a fool kiss you and never...
...let a kiss fool kiss. (Joey Adams)

If grass can grow through cement...
...love can find you at any time in your life. (Cher)

The heart has no wrinkles. (movie title)

The head never rules the heart but just...
...becomes its partner in crime. (Mignon McLaughlin)

Love is a game that...
...two can play and both win. (Eva Gabor)

Love is friendship set on fire. (Jeremy Taylor)

Love is a friendship set to music. (Joseph Campbell)

We are all mortal until the first kiss...
...and the second glass of wine. (Eduardo Galeano)

Never forget the nine most important words...
...in any marriage: I love you, you are beautiful, please forgive me. (H. Jackson Brown, Jr.)

Sometimes you miss the memories and not...

...the person. (source unknown)

It's better to have loved and lost than...
...to do forty pounds of laundry a week. (Laurence J. Peter)

They say every day is a gift but...
...why does it have to be more laundry? (source unknown)

Slogans (10)

It's your world, take control (AMX)

Dreams made real (Agilent)

Discover what's possible (Anritsu)

Get in the game (ATI Technologies)

How big can you dream? (Cadence)

The possibilities are infinite (Fujitsu)

Pushing limits (Rohde and Schwarz)

The power of dreams (Honda)

Just do it (Nike)

Make the most of now (Vodaphone)

Command Headlines (30)

Let's meet in our dreams tonight

Answer this question...

Pause a moment, stranger…

Teach me how to dance

Stop everything!

Help me out here!

Let me rescue you

Read this now

Don't just let life happen. Create a life.

Don't give up yet

Let me introduce you to someone special – me

Don't make me hold my breath any longer!

Take a risk

Jump into life

Join the adventure

Escape the mundane

Rush into joy

Let me capture your heart

Read on and I'll transform your life

Embrace this opportunity

I'll bring the picnic, you bring the smile

Read this or I'll shoot my porcupine…

Time sensitive material. Open immediately!

Try this next time you're blue…

Let me introduce you to…

Do one thing every day that scares you

Forget that loser!

Well, don't just sit there!

Seek and ye shall find

Let me explain something

Testimonial Headlines (9)

Experts concur that…

90% of all professional skiers believe…

Voted most fun because…

Every girl I've ever dated agrees…

All my friends say…

Dogs and cats adore me because…

Voted most likely to…

In a unanimous vote I was…

In a recent comparison…

Headlines Plus the First Paragraph (30)

Here are several samples of various headlines followed by the first paragraph. You'll see how the first paragraph ties in with the headline, yet also begins a more personal introduction.

It's better to have loved and lost than…

…do forty pounds of laundry a week. Plus running a household, raising three kids two dogs and the occasional hamster, and keeping it all within a strict budget. I wouldn't trade those memories for anything but I'm always eager to make new ones.

Once or twice a year I provide…

…a safe and nurturing foster home for local pets. It's hard on me because I hate to give them up. But it's my little way of 'paying it forward'. I wonder what the world would be like if everyone tried to do that.

In a unanimous vote I was…

…chosen best mommy in the world by my 4-year-old twins. It's a heavy burden, what with all the competition out there, but I work very hard 24/7 to live up to such high expectations. As you've figured out I'm a single mother with her hands full but there's still a piece of the puzzle missing, and much more joy to share.

Tired of another Sunday afternoon…

…spent folding clothes? Me, too. I'd rather be playing miniature golf or scarfing a Sundae at
Baskin Robbins. Watching a comedy movie if it's raining. Or maybe playing scrabble (warning: I'm pretty good).

Have you ever laughed so hard that…

…tears ran down your leg? Well, maybe they weren't tears but never mind. If you're looking for someone with a great sense of humor, that's me. If you're looking for intelligence, creativity, and wit, that's me. If you're looking for loyalty, compassion and sensitivity, well, what a coincidence!

Where do I go to collect smiles?…

…Movies. Circus. Pet shop. Weddings. Friend's house. Ocean. Mountains. River. Woods. Road trip. Walking. Dancing. Museums. Volunteering. Fairs. Festivals. Concerts. Plays. Comedy clubs. Sidewalk cafes. Halloween parties. Playing cards. Shooting pool. Reading.

They say every day is a gift but…

…why does laundry pile up so fast? When I was growing up I read a lot of science fiction and no one ever mentioned a laundromat in any spaceship. I figured they had some futuristic fabric that repelled stains and always stayed fresh. I could use that for my gym shoes, too.

I'm not sure what I am…

…but other people have said funny, smart, honest, and optimistic. There's more, I'm sure. But what will we talk about later?

If I had a million bucks for every…

…time I dreamed of you we'd be rich. So what would you like to do with all that money? Travel? Open a cool business? Live on the beach? Sail around the world?

My promise to you…

I'll always respect you in all that you do. I'll call you my partner and equal in life. When you're weak I'll be strong. When you're sad I'll find you joy. When you're timid I'll be brave. When you need support you'll have all of mine. My heart will give you love like no other. And all that I have in this world will be yours.

Click here to read your horoscope…

Your life has been unsettled lately because of Pluto's influence over the rings of Saturn. As Orion ascends and overshadows the Milky Way blessings of great significance approach. The stars align in your favor and you will soon meet someone wonderful. It could be me.

A man's reach should exceed his grasp.

Know what I mean? It's about having a purpose in life. Setting worthwhile goals and attempting to achieve them. But it's really about the journey and not the ultimate destination.

Ever drifted down a river at dawn?

The rising sun sets each dew drop sparkling sharp as a diamond. Something out of sight splashes into the water. Leaves rustle from an invisible breeze. And all of nature dreamily awakens to enjoy a new day. A day full of wonderful promise because right now everything's possible.

And then my head exploded!…

See, I had just broken up with my significant other so all my friends and family rallied around to help. Everyone had some particular advice: Get out and date again! Take some you time! Go on a vacation! Move to another city! Hire a mafia hit man! Exercise! Cry it out! Walk it out! And the voices went on and on and got louder and shriller until all I could hear was this chitter chatter babble blabble blahbity blahbity blah and then without warning my head exploded.

Pick a number. Any number…

…was it two? Of course it was. Because two implies you and someone special. And maybe that someone special is me. Or it could be a cuddly new kitten. But for the moment let's assume it's me. Here's why it should be:

I've reached that comfortable stage…

… in life where I don't have to impress people. I've been around the block. I've experienced some great adventures. And my friends are loyal and true.

What would happen if you passed gas…

…in a spacesuit? It would be the worst kind of toot ever: you couldn't deny it, you couldn't escape it, and the smell would stay with you all the way back to the space station. I don't guess Captain Kirk ever had to worry about it. And Spock would call it illogical.

I spent both the saddest and happiest day…

…volunteering for MDA last month. Sad to see what this terrible disease does, but happy because we raised over fifteen hundred dollars for research. So we're that much closer to a cure.

Last month I discovered a…

…small, cozy, family-owned restaurant with only six tables. They serve Italian, my favorite, and offer an inexpensive but excellent Chianti. I went alone and it was great. I don't mind dining by myself but I also enjoy the company of someone special.

Last month I went biking in the…

…mountains. My fourth trip and, as always, just wonderful. The fresh air, the towering pines, the golden sunshine, and what a great workout I got without even knowing it.

Well this is fun. NOT.

Because I don't know what to say. I feel like I'm interviewing for a new job. So here's my resume: smart, energetic, multi-task oriented, works well with others, good communication skills, consensus builder, team player, and promises never to steal extra pens or paper clips.

Ever felt like you're in a movie?

Except instead of being one of the stars you're the half-wit sidekick who's always taken for granted and never gets the co-star but lives a virtuous and honest life while everyone else finds treasure and happiness and love and wins the lottery and… Well, enough of that!

Last week I got caught in the…

…rain while riding my motorcycle. And I had forgotten my rain gear. So I pulled over to a convenience store and bought a box of large garbage bags. That's right, I made a poncho out of one bag and wrapped my boots in a couple others. It wasn't much fun then but makes for a great story now.

The day I broke up with normal…

…I had a fling with insanity. Intense. Full throttle. Exciting. Dangerous. But now that's off my 'to do' list and it's back to merely being interesting, amusing, intelligent, balanced, spiritual, adventurous, creative, joyous, and modest.

Dear potential match…

…are you looking as hard for me as I am for you? Are you eager to experience fresh adventures and explore new roads? Are you smart, creative, independent and still young at heart? Are you ready to embrace life at full throttle? Then keep reading.

5 secrets no one knows about me…

… 1) I love dancing in the rain; 2) I still believe in magic; 3) Sometimes I write poetry in library books; 4) I am so much more than the life I lead; 5) I love the suspense of falling in love.

90% of all professional skiers believe…

…Jackson Hole is the very best place for catching big air or bombing. Not that I do much of either, but I enjoy a long day carving through the powder followed by an evening of hot chocolate in front of a roaring fire.

More fun than your ex…

…smarter, too. Add in wittier, gentler, more secure and a much better sense of humor.   Did I mention more modest? Well, six out of seven is good, right? But enough about me. Let's talk about you.

Stop Everything!...

...Stop everything for a couple moments and tell me what's most important in your life. Finding a solid, rewarding, caring relationship, of course, because that's why you're here. Establishing trust, friendship, and rapport because that's part of all good relationships. And then, hopefully, planning, designing and building a wonderful new future together.

What are you doing here?!

I can't believe someone as cool as you is looking around this site. But I'm glad you stopped by to read my profile. I think you'll like what you see so let me tell you more.

Powerful Calls To Action (26)

Interested? Shoot me a line.

Let me know if you felt a spark.

Email me and let's see what happens.

The next step is up to you. What are you waiting for?

Time is short. Contact me.

If you've read this far I know you're interested. Let me know.

The first step is the hardest. Take it now.

Get in touch now.

Email me now.

What are you waiting for?

You know what to do next.

Don't wait any longer.

Take the next important step now.

Act now.

Why wait any longer?

You know you want to.

Start now.

I can't wait to hear from you.

Now reach for your keyboard.

I invite you to contact me.

Take the first step now.

Go ahead and pull the trigger.

Why not take the next step?

If you've read this far then take the next step and contact me.

Take a chance – you'll be glad you did.

We're not getting any younger – write back now.

Putting It All Together (50)

Alright, I've already provided you with hundreds of great ways to energize your personal ad, but now here are 50 complete examples to help kickstart your creative juices. Feel free to use any, all or part of them – or let them help inspire you to create something as totally unique and wonderful as you are.

I'm positive you'll start getting more and better responses by utilizing all the powerful techniques in this eBook. I can't say when you'll meet that special someone, but I sincerely hope it's soon. In fact, I'm betting on it because you've now got that competitive edge that will help you really stand out in the crowded world of online dating.

Good luck!

Once or twice a year I provide…

…a safe and nurturing foster home for local pets. It's hard on me because I hate to give them up. But it's my little way of 'paying it forward'. I wonder what the world would be like if everyone tried to do that.

But it's not something I stress out about. I work hard during the week in staff support. I play hard during the weekend. And sometimes I just relax really hard. Golfing is my newest pastime but my handicap is mid-triple digit. I'm a fair bowler and if it's nice outside you'll find me hiking the local nature trail. I sometimes participate in weekend-long book-reading or movie-watching marathons, but they better be really good.

As for who I'd like to meet, well, I'm open. Finding someone who is looking for a serious relationship would be good. Someone willing to try new adventures. Someone smart and funny is high on my list, too. If you've read this far that's good, it means you're interested. So email me and we'll see what happens then.

I spent both the saddest and happiest day...

...volunteering for MDA last summer. Sad to see what this terrible disease does, but happy because we raised over fifteen hundred dollars for research. So we're that much closer to a cure.

I like to stay active, whether it's volunteering within the community or participating in one of my clubs. Let's see, some of my favorite clubs involve Dining Out, Kayaking, Stage Acting and Civil War Reenactments. I consider watching the sun set with a glass of wine a nice activity, too.

Now it's time to list what I'd like in an ideal match. Oh my! So many ideas, so little space. But here goes: creative, witty, strong character, kind, open to new ideas, gentle, able to leap tall buildings in one bound. OK, that last one is negotiable.

So are you up to the task? I certainly am. Now drop me a line.

Last month I discovered a...

...small, cozy, family-owned restaurant with only ten tables. They serve Italian, my favorite, and offer an inexpensive but excellent Chianti. I went alone and it was great. I don't mind dining by myself but I also enjoy the company of someone special.

What makes someone special to me? Well, now that my kids have left I'm free to take off on a moment's notice for a weekend at the coast or mountains. How about you? I'm mature enough that I don't need any extra drama. I'll be retiring in six years and then

I'd like to pull up roots and just explore, even if it's just for a few weeks now and then. I don't mind travelling alone but I also know the joy of sharing life with someone special. I hope it's you.

But even the longest journey starts with a single step. You know what to do next.

Last week I went biking in the...

...mountains. My fourth trip and, as always, just wonderful. The fresh air was electric, the smell of the great pines was like smoky perfume, and what a great workout I got without even knowing it.

If I had my choice of jobs it would be Park Ranger so I could be in the woods all the time. But instead I'm a sales manager, a position I worked my way up to from stock clerk. So now you know I'm smart and hard-working

So what about you? Do you like being outdoors on the weekends? Woods, beach, mountains, it makes no difference to me. Do you like unexpected adventures? Spur-of-the-moment road trips? Holding hands in front of the TV?

If you answered yes to even one question we have something in common. Maybe we have more.

Get in touch and let's find out.

The other week I got caught in the...

...rain while riding my motorcycle. And I had forgotten my rain gear. So I pulled over to a convenience store and bought a box of large garbage bags. That's right, I made a poncho out of one bag and wrapped my boots in a couple others. It wasn't much fun then but makes for a great story now.

I'm looking to make more great stories with someone exceptional. You don't have to ride behind me on my Harley, but how about the beach, especially in the Spring? I like the mountains, too, in the fall when the air is crisp and cool and the leaves are just turning colors. But I can be perfectly content relaxing with a good book or watching a DVD.

Life's a trip and every day is special. But like me, you're the type who knows that some days start out sunny and then turn rainy. But you know how to go with the flow. You're a free spirit with a streak of independence who's in search of someone to stand with and not behind.

Care to share the ride?

More fun than your ex...

...smarter, too. Add in wittier, gentler, more secure and a much better sense of humor.   Did I mention more modest? Well, six out of seven is good, right? But enough about me. Let's talk about you.

You're smart, adventurous, amusing and fun to be around, too. With all that going you don't worry about modesty, you're the real deal and proud of it. So let me tell you all the fun things we can do together:

Road trips on a drizzly day. Strolling along the marina on a crisp, fall afternoon. Watching a silver crescent moon rise over an inky blue ocean. Lounging around a small table in a dark pub listening to an acoustical trio. A cut-throat game of Putt Putt.

So more about me, you say.

OK. To begin with I've reached a comfortable stage in life and know who I am and where I'm going. I'm bright and creative and curious. I'm a free spirit. I enjoy laughing and hearing others laugh. I'm loyal. Trusting. Honest. Faithful. I like riding my Harley occasionally. But I'm all for other cool adventures. I'm self-employed with a couple of businesses; writing is one, managing rental property is another. For the most part my time is my own to shape as I please. I very much like that. I'd very much like to share that.

Still reading? Feeling a little interested?

That's good because it means there's already something between us. Let's see if it grows.

Shoot me an email.

Sandboxes aren't just for kids....

Take my sandbox for instance. It's pretty big, miles and miles long. Burn-your-feet hot in the summer. Cold and shivery in the winter. One side borders some pretty deep water, the ocean, actually. Condos and restaurants and the boardwalk run along the other side.

I go there to play every time I get the chance. Any weather. It's always beautiful, always different.

So where else do I like to play? Quiet museums, just about any one of them. The mountains when fall paints the leaves in dark rainbow colors. Maybe playing cards on a gray rainy day. Reading a good book is like playing to me, too. But I can have fun just about anywhere.

So what about you? What kind of sandbox do you like to play in?

Let me know.

Ever eaten bugs?

Have you ever raced down the highway riding your bicycle on a fresh Spring morning under a hot blue sky past farms and fields and woods as the bright yellow sun shines down and you're rushing along so fast the fresh wind forces your face into a great big smile as you speed on into sweeping curves that promise wonderful new adventures right around the bend? Yeah, you know what I mean by eating bugs, but it just doesn't matter because life is so incredibly large and shiny and there you are right in the middle of the fantastic now.

I wish I could do that every day but to pay my bills I work as an engineer. Which I enjoy, but I know the value of my off time, too, and I like to spend it outside. Kayaking, hiking, tennis, softball, you get the picture, I'm high energy and like to stay active.

So tell me about yourself. Are you looking to race down some country highway, watch the sun set over the river, enjoy a brisk game of tennis?

Well, I just served the ball into your court, and I'm waiting for you to hit it back.

The dishes can wait because right now…

…the bright morning sun is drying the dew off the grass, a gentle breeze ruffles the yellow daisies in my yard, the sky sizzles with an electrical blue, and somewhere, somehow, somewhen you are reading this.

And just who are you, you wonder? Do you remember the movie 'Dirty Dancing' when Baby said: "I'm scared of walking out of this room and never feeling the rest of my whole life the way I feel when I'm with you." Well, that's who you are and that's who I want to be for you.

And no, I don't live my life through the movies, but I know a good line when I hear one. Sure, I'm a romantic, but isn't that just another word for faith? That good things happen to good people? That life is full of miracles?

So forget the dirty dishes you should be doing. What you should do right now is write me back.

Is it just me, or…

…does it seem like most people don't have a clue? You know the ones I'm talking about, they can't see the forest for the trees, or they define themselves by what they do for a living, or maybe they just don't realize there's so much more to life than a gamebox or a smartphone.

Well good for them, I say. But it's not me. I value life by every little breath I savor, or the serenity I feel gazing at a pale mist rising over a lake, or the wordless wonder I experience with every powerful thunder storm.

My friends call me a free spirit, and I think it scares them a little, that I place more value in a field of blooming orange sunflowers than on the newest fashions. When they ask me about it I tell them if I have to explain, well, they wouldn't understand.

But you get it, don't you? Like me you're not looking to leave a trail so much as create a path. Toward what? Well, that's a question two can answer as well as one.

Reach out, I'm waiting.

Tell the truth, wouldn't you rather…

…be sitting in Paris right now, sipping a saucy merlot under the awning of a sidewalk café, casually watching the tourists walk past? Then a sudden spring rain pours down, washing the streets and reflecting back the warm lights from the local shops. Then just as suddenly the rain stops and maybe it's time to stroll along the Left Bank, watching the working boats ply their trade on the cool waters.

I've never done that, but it's on my bucket list. Renting an RV and exploring America is on my list. Improving my golf game. Taking another Caribbean cruise. And finding someone to share all that with.

I bet you've got a great bucket list, too. I'd love to hear it and see what we share in common. But I already know one thing we have in common – a desire to share life's adventures with that one special someone.

Let's get started.

I own two rescue dogs that are…

… spoiled rotten. If you looked into their dark brown eyes you'd know why. I can't make up for their rotten past but I can try and give them a wonderful now. Just trying to save the world in my own way, I guess, one small step at a time.

Ever noticed how pure in spirit animals are? Dogs love you for who you are and not how you look. Cats love you in their own way but on their own terms. Fish are a huge responsibility because you're like some god taking care of their little world. Rabbits don't let on how smart they are. I'm not much on snakes or birds or gerbils or turtles or baby ducks, but I've had them all and liked them at the time. I had a friend once with two monkeys who were just totally nasty and obnoxious. Don't need to go there again.

But I'll always share part of my life with animal companions. They make my world larger and more complete. I'm about more than just that, of course, in so many ways. So maybe we share a few things in common. If so let me know. It would be a good start.

Stop Everything!

Stop everything for a couple moments and tell me what's most important in your life. Finding a solid, rewarding, caring relationship, of course, because that's why you're here. Establishing trust, friendship, and rapport because that's part of all good relationships. And then, hopefully, planning, designing and building a wonderful new future together.

Good thing you're reading this because that's what I'm looking for, too.

Now allow me to introduce myself.

I'm five years out of college with my Masters in Sociology. I like helping people and have established a very rewarding career in a growing field. But I'm looking for more. I want the joy of a long-term relationship and to discover the wonderful blessings of raising a family.

So I've decided to cast a wide net in my search. I'm very active in various social settings and charities. I like to get out every weekend on a road trip, maybe to some museum, or even just to a flea market or the movie theater around the corner. I've just joined a great group for Young Professionals and a Dining Out group so I'm meeting great new people every day.

Which is why I'm here online, to make sure I don't pass up any opportunity to meet my special match. Is it you? Boy, I sure hope so because I'm ready to create the next exciting chapter in our life. Please contact me soon.

P.S. I've just volunteered to help with the upcoming Renaissance Fair, which raises money for MDA. I'll be dressed as the Court Jester. What would you dress as?

I promised my goldfish that…

…I'd stop paying so much attention to the dog. He gets jealous (my goldfish, I mean). My dog's a Labrador and pretty laid back so he's cool. But take my word there's nothing worse than a goldfish green with envy.

You can't please everybody, as I'm sure you know. But if you please yourself you'll probably also please the people you care about. And if they're not pleased that you're pleased then why are they in your life?

So, I'm two years out of college and an elementary teacher. I love my kids, which means I love my job. I get my summers off and spent the last one as a camp counselor. That was a blast. I think maybe next summer I'd like to travel. Don't quite know where yet.

I'm looking for a gentleman, emphasis on 'gentle'. Someone quietly confident who doesn't need to be the center of attention. Bonus points for intelligence. Extra bonus points if you're a teacher so we both get our summers off. And five gold stars if you play a musical instrument. I play the flute.

Let me know if you're interested. We'll deal with the goldfish later.

I'm having trouble…

…describing myself so I asked my best friend for a testimonial. Here's what she said: "Don't pass up a chance to meet this extraordinary woman. Whenever she walks into a room she lights it up with her shining smile and keen wit. Children and small animals adore her, handsome movie stars stutter helplessly in her presence, and once when it started raining she walked outside and a rainbow appeared at her feet. All that's missing is the gentleman with her glass slipper."

Well, now you know why she's my best friend, and who am I to deny her wonderful observations?

But I'll fill in a few of the gaps. I work in sales so you know I'm enthusiastic and outgoing. I enjoy spending lazy weekends sitting by the surf reading the latest book by Nicholas Sparks. I like most all movies except ones that scare me. I've memorized three recipes so if you know four we'll eat something different each day of the week. I'm allergic to cat hair.

Wow, doesn't that sound just a little dull? So go back and read the testimonial again. When you've finished reading contact me immediately if you have my missing glass slipper.

Instead of sleeping in this weekend wouldn't you...

...rather hit half a dozen yard sales and maybe find some way-cool treasures? I once found an old watch I sold on eBay for forty bucks (cost me five). And I have a set of power tools I fixed up which I use making furniture. That's my weekend hobby.

I'm what they call a low-maintenance lady. I don't need the big city to find stuff to do. I like watching comedies on TV, or the nature channel, or just sitting in my shed working with wood. I made both rocking chairs on my front porch. I'm handy that way.

Do you have critters? Dogs? Cats? Chickens? I do. They mostly just wandered up and decided to stay. They earn their living. Watchdog. Mouse hunter. Egg layers. Companionship.

So what are you doing this weekend? Sleeping in, or something more fun? If you have some ideas write me back.

There I was, minding my own business when...

...I suddenly had this vision of you: smart, funny, quirky, creative, spontaneous, adventurous, kind, caring and loving.

Am I right? Oh wait, I forgot how you like the feel of hot sand under your bare feet, how rainy days sometimes make you sad and happy at the same time, and why you like old cartoons on TV.

You're curious and a bit adventurous, too. That's why you're here, not that you have to be, I know you've got plenty of friends you enjoy spending time with. But you're not going to take a chance of someone like me slipping past just because we didn't cross paths at the Jazz Festival.

OK, so now what? It's easy, just get in touch. Seize the moment, as they say. The rest will take care of itself.

5 secrets no one knows about me:

1) I love dancing in the rain

2) I still believe in magic

3) Sometimes I write poetry in library books

4) I am so much more than the life I lead

5) I love the suspense of falling in love

So what about you? What are some of your secrets? Did you ever pee in the ocean? Not answer the door when you were happy alone? Create a separate Twitter account so you could complain about what's really bothering you?

You can share with me, I won't tell. Well, I might if it turns out you're a super-villain intent on world domination and the total destruction of rainbows and sunsets. Or you don't like unicorns, that's a deal-breaker, too.

But don't wait to let me know. Let's work on some secrets together.

Does Spooning Lead To Forking?...

...yes, if the right spork is there. OK, stop groaning. All I really wanted to do was get your attention so I could introduce myself. Ready? Here goes:

I have a sense of humor and love to laugh. I remember the last *Austin Powers* movie I saw where this teenager in the next row laughed so hard he snorked his soda. I nearly fell out of my seat. I can laugh at myself, too, and why not? Life is serious enough.

Myself, I believe life is about finding joy wherever you can, and how can you laugh without finding joy? And isn't that why we're here? The answer, of course, is yes.

Now for the dull part where I tell you all about me. Oh, never mind. Let's save it for an email. You get to ask two questions, so make them good. And then you have to answer two of my questions.

Fire away.

What should I do next?

Now that my kids are grown and I'm happily retired I fill my new freedom with all kinds of unexpected adventures. Last week I discovered this great Oriental restaurant and, on a dare, ate sushi for the very first time. It wasn't half bad! Several months ago I joined a square dance club and twice a month we get together and kick up our heels. I regularly attend the University adventure film series, although you won't catch me personally exploring the dangerous jungles of Borneo!

So what about you? Are you still young at heart? Maybe not so eager to go tornado chasing but up for a day's drive down the coast? And I'm thinking of taking up golf. We could learn together or if you're experienced you could help me learn.

It all sounds so fun, doesn't it? Now tell me what you'd like to do next.

P.S. The rumors about me taking up hot air ballooning are still just rumors. Unless it's something you'd like to try with me. What do you think?

My Boat Is Sinking. Can You Help?

It's just a 22-foot day sailor and I'm pretty sure it's properly patched, but I need someone to steer while I keep an eye on the bilge levels.

Do you like sailing? I just discovered it since I retired two years ago and it's a terrific way to combine fun and adventure. If you've never sailed before don't worry, I'll show you the ropes (sorry, couldn't resist that little joke). And if you are experienced then I sure could use a good first mate.

I'm not just about sailing, though. I like driving the Blue Ridge Parkway in the fall when the leaves burn crimson and gold. If you've never been put it on your 'to do' list. I know you'd like it. But don't forget a jacket because the evenings can turn very chilly.

So how am I doing so far? I mean, have I sparked your interest enough to chat?

Go ahead and email me. No telling what else we share in common.

Ever hiked A Mountain Trail In Spring?

The air is crisp and fresh, birds warble, trees rustle in the wind, and the high white clouds scamper across the sharp blue sky like little fuzzy sheep. Can you picture that in your mind? It's a wonderful thing to share with someone, don't you think?

I call that a good weekend. Same with driving to the beach and lazing through the day on a towel listening to the roaring surf. Then again if it's raining I enjoy strolling through some cool museum. Or even just wandering a bookstore in search of some new author.

As for what I do for a living I'm self-employed. I drive a vending route collecting the money and keeping the machines filled with snacks. It's what I do, not who I am. But I certainly like being my own boss and working my own schedule.

But on weekends and holidays, oh my, that's when the real me jumps out. Smart, fun, energetic, adventurous, playful, fun. And always open to new things.

So when's the last time you set up a picnic by a cold rushing mountain stream? And what kind of sandwiches would you like me to bring?

Let me know.

Do The Neighbors Call The Cops On You?

They did once on me when I hosted the most kick-butt Halloween costume party this side of the Mississippi River. The cops were cool, although they sure paid a lot of attention to the girl wearing nothing but body paint. I was a Roman centurion.

Other than that I'm pretty straight and laid back. No speeding tickets even, well, just that one last year when I was late for work. I'm a night manager at the bowling alley so I get to play for free. I enjoy it during the winter when it's so cold outside. When the weather's warmer I like being outside, maybe messing around my yard. I grow my own vegetables, cukes, tomatoes, beans, squash, green peppers, watermelons, stuff like that.

Hey, am I making you hungry talking about garden-fresh produce? Well I can solve that fast enough.

Write me.

Is Your Cat Plotting To Kill You?

Sometimes I think my cat is plotting to kill me, especially when he walks between my ankles just as I start down the stairs. But then he realizes no one would feed him or empty his cat box. So I get to live another day, unless he finds a new owner.

One reason I like my cat is because I can go away for the weekend with no problems. Mostly I go camping because it fits my budget. And there's nothing like lounging around a toasty campfire with good friends. We're in the middle of the world's longest-running gin rummy game.

So now you know a few things I like to do for fun. What else? I like to visit the mall and watch people. Man, have I seen some real cases. I like shooting pool, and I'm halfway good. Once in a while I go dancing with my buddies.

I work as a cashier but I don't call that fun, just a way to pay my bills. I attend night school three times a week. In one more year I'll be an RN. Woohoo!

That's me in a nutshell. Interested? Drop me a line.

What Are Your Plans This Weekend?

If it involves tossing your bathing suit and towel into the car and heading for the beach then we have something fun in common.

What else might we have in common? Well, I'm a drummer in a local band so I like rock 'n' roll. I'm assistant chef at a pretty good restaurant so I like food. You already know I like the beach. I like sleeping in on Sunday mornings. Unless I'm headed for the beach. Which I like any time of the year.

Now it's your turn. I'm sure we have much more in common.

Let me know.

I'm a single dad with too much...

...spare time on his hands. OK, that's a big fib. But I could write the expert's guide on intergalactic time management and multi-dimensional multi-tasking. I picked those terms up from my 10-year-old boy's science fiction books. I encourage my kids to read. Like someone once said, 'Reading is a discount ticket to everywhere'. My 12-year-old daughter is on another voyage in finding herself. So far we've done acting classes, dance, piano, soccer and yoga. I encourage her to experiment to her heart's desire, within reason of course.

By day I work as an accountant. All other times I'm chauffeur, chef, homework advisor, laundry sorter, and Mr. Meany when it comes to watching too much TV and bedtime. However, I do host some legendary sleepovers. The last one involved every *Star Wars* movie ever made, no bedtime, and an unlimited supply of ice cream, chips, and decaf sodas.

In truth I have a very blessed and rewarding life, which I'd very much like to share with one extraordinary person. You'll know if it's you.

But hurry! My son's building a positronic temporal spatial discombobulator and there's no telling what planet we'll be on next week!

I am, you are, together so much more.

10 facts about me:

1. I make up songs to sing in the shower.

2. I still miss the dog I grew up with.

3. I like to bake bread for friends.

4. I love the energy of a big city.

5. I have a goofy streak.

6. I blew up the engine to my first car.

7. I would like to skydive some day.

8. I lived in France as an exchange student.

9. I have a free spirit.

10. I am searching for a true heart.

You have a career you enjoy and plans for the future. You want to share life with a true friend and equal partner. You know how to give and receive joy. Honesty and integrity are important. You are a good person in search of a good person.

No winks or likes. If you're interested just email.

Ever watched a storm at the beach?

So have you ever watched a storm roll in over the ocean? First the dark clouds gather thickly and everything fades to gray. Out on the water the chop kicks up and foamy whitecaps prance around. Then you see a wall of dark rain rushing forward and hopefully by then you're under cover. When the rain suddenly hits the ocean hisses loudly and the sand spatters and puffs on the beach. Not a bird or a crab or a tourist can be seen, they've all taken shelter. It's a glorious, singular, rare kind of beauty and a wonderful thing to share.

So what are some other wonderful things to share? Laughter. Wonder. Adventure. Passion. Serenity. Books like "The Artist's Way" or "Conversations With God". A movie like "Hugo". Cold evenings in front of warm fires. A walk on the beach in the rain. Quiet drives heading nowhere. And hearts, of course, hearts are wonderful to share with that one special someone.

As for me I've reached a comfortable stage in life and know who I am and where I'm going. People describe me as smart and creative with a wide sense of humor. Loyal. Trusting. Honest and faithful. I like riding my Harley. I'm self-employed with a couple of businesses; landscaping is one, managing rental property is another.

I'm heading back to the beach soon to watch the rain and savor the beauty. Kind of recharges my battery, reminds me of how grand and beautiful life can be, especially when it's shared with someone special.

If it's you shoot me a line. Maybe watching the next storm roll in could be the start of something wonderful.

Have you ever been so broke...

…you had to live under a bridge eating old french fries tossed out of car windows and drinking soda from a can someone used as an ash tray? Well neither have I and that's a good thing.

So what are some other good things? The innocence of babies. The crack of thunder just before dawn. Afternoons spent fishing in the river. Sharing quiet times while it rains.

As you can see from my picture I'm a pilot. What I'd really like to be is a writer. I'm almost finished with my first book, a comic adventure about, well, a pilot. A lot of the stuff in the book really happened but I've changed all the names and places. I think it's a pretty funny book, and I know it would make a great movie.

Speaking of great movies, I'm looking for someone to be my co-star in life. I can promise you fun, travel, commitment, honesty, and a life full of joy and happiness.

Email and make your reservation now.

How To Set Your Toes On Fire

So what's the best way to set your toes on fire? I like to start out early, after a good breakfast. Then I toss some clothes in my bag, toothbrush, razor, change of socks, you get the idea. Throw it all in the back of my car. Jump behind the wheel and head east.

Sometimes I'll stop in Bay City for some steamed oysters. I know this great little restaurant downtown with a laid-back atmosphere and some really great food. Seafood not your favorite? No problem, they've got all the standard fare and an excellent Cobb Salad.

Back on the road. Notice how the air subtly changes? Crisp. Tangy. A touch of salt. We're getting close.

I hate the traffic. But that's the price. Lots to listen to on Sirius, though. I like the 50s station, or E-Street, maybe I'll even listen to Rush for giggles.

Finally I get to spin the wheel right and head up and over the bridge and suddenly the sparkling sound is below me and further out the azure ocean shines and twinkles like a huge blue diamond. This is where I open my sunroof and symbolically toss out all my troubles and tribulations. Man, you can't help but smile on the island.

More traffic but all my windows are down so I can hear the roaring breakers not far off. Then soon enough I pull off the main drag and up to my place. Dash in. Throw on my trunks. Grab a beach towel and I'm back out the door.

Not far to the beach. Listen to those gulls squealing up above. Feel that hot sun beating down. Did I forget my sunblock? Who cares.

I stake out my patch of sand. Snap open my beach towel. Slip off my sneakers and head for the water.

Yeeeouch that sand is hot! My feet are on fire! My toes about to burst into flame! I'm running now. Heading for the cool salt ocean. Leaving smoking footprints behind. Just another few steps!

But that's the very best way I know to set my toes on fire. So what about you? Got a better idea? Let me hear back. Let's kindle a fire together.

3 Wishes For You

If I could grant you 3 wishes what would they be?

Love, of course. For Love is the completion of ourselves. To be loved simply for who we are validates our essential worth. Whether from the love of a puppy or a child or a parent or hopefully our one and true life's mate – we are reassured that our very existence enriches the world.

Wish Number 2 would be Serenity. To know peace in our journey, both during times of ease and times of struggle. Serenity implies faith: faith in a benign universe and a loving creator and realizing that from faith springs happiness. But knowing, too, that until happiness arrives our feet will steadily move us forward and the serenity we carry will smooth our way and lighten our burdens.

And finally, Joy. For from the Love we give and receive, and from the Serenity that floats us calmly along the river of life, from these two blessings flow Joy: The Joy of our existence, the Joy of this moment, and the Joy of each simple breath as a renewal of the splendor of our being.

And those are my wishes for you, good Traveler. May your journey overflow with an abundance of blessings and spiritual riches.

Reach out to me.

Rare commodity seeks rare commodity

I'm a rare commodity seeking a rare commodity. A free spirit. Smart and creative. Humorous. Sensual. Loving. Caring.

I don't love halfway and you don't either. Passion becomes us. We fill ourselves with the joy of each other without losing our selves.

We celebrate the union of us yet know other joys. Each of us enriches the other and enriches the world. We are strong together and strong apart. Together we exist in trust and safety, for we know how to nurture love.

We are young at heart yet wise from experience. Past scars have faded. We know that giving is receiving. We admire and desire each other. We are friends, lovers, companions and mischievous hooligans.

Our time is fleeting.

Come seize this moment with me.

Life should not be a journey to...

...the grave with the intention of arriving safely in a pretty and well preserved body, but rather to skid in broadside in a cloud of smoke, thoroughly used up, totally worn out, and loudly proclaiming "Wow! What a Ride!"

We're only here once. Don't you agree? Set here to walk along this strange and awesome path. To live life fully, experience adventure, breathe in joy, find love, maybe lose love, maybe find love again.

Sometimes I'm scared. I admit it. But I'm surrounded by good friends and good memories and the belief that more good times and friends are in store. And for all of this I'm grateful.

So tell me what you're grateful for. What adventures are you seeking? What brings you joy? Are you searching for someone to walk beside you on this path called life?

Maybe we'll click. Wouldn't that be nice? Maybe we won't click. But nothing ventured, nothing gained.

Still, all the best journeys start with just one step. Take it now and contact me.

Where do you go to collect smiles?

Here's where I go: Movies. Circus. Pet shop. Weddings. Friend's house. Ocean. Mountains. River. Woods. Road trip. Walking. Dancing. Museums. Volunteering. Fairs. Festivals. Concerts. Plays. Comedy clubs. Sidewalk cafes. Halloween parties. Playing cards. Shooting pool. Reading.

Now you tell me.

Medicine, law, business, engineering, these are...

... noble pursuits and necessary to sustain life. But poetry, beauty, romance, love, these are what we stay alive for. (Dead Poets Society).

When I heard Robin Williams say that in the movie it took my breath away. Because isn't it true? I mean, I like my job, but I don't live for it. What I live for are the moments that take my breath away. It might be the poetry of a secluded waterfall deep in the woods. Or the beauty of a sudden double rainbow after a booming thunderstorm. And then there's love, and romance, and sharing it all with that special someone.

Isn't that why you're here? To find those special moments and maybe that special someone who will take your breath away. It's certainly why I'm here.

Let's give it a shot.

Read this or I'll shoot my porcupine…

OK, I don't really have a porcupine and I'd never shoot anything live, but honestly, I'm getting tired of all the jerks out there. Please don't be one because I'll recognize you instantly.

So let's go over the ground rules: you're not married or a player; you're over your ex already; you don't smoke or drink like a fish; you have a job and a car; I'll know you if we meet because your picture isn't ten years old; and you're a nice person.

Am I being picky? Or maybe prickly? You bet because my time is valuable. Still with me? Great, because I'm serious about finding someone special.

So what are you looking for? Witty, smart and creative? That's me. Cleans up well but doesn't mind getting dirty fingernails? Me, again. Enjoys a good movie or some TV but really loves the awesome beauty of nature? You've got me pegged.

There's more if you're interested. You know what to do next. But I swear if you're a jerk I'll feed you to my porcupine.

Dear Cupid…

…why does it seem so difficult at times? Here I am, walking along this beautiful path we call life, and I'm still searching for that special someone.

Let me explain some things. I'm mature and responsible with an excellent career. My kids are grown and I have the house to myself. I'm financially sound with no debts to pay. I'm a few pounds overweight but I'm working on that. I bowl and golf and know my way around a pool table. I'm the regular guy next door.

Now let me ask you a few things, Cupid. They say there's a match for everyone. Please don't tell me mine is ten thousand miles away in China. You know I'm not looking for a Playboy model, but not a couch potato, either.

Is it asking too much for smart, funny and independent? Someone who's over the past and ready to explore a new future? Someone who enjoys the finer things in life: dining, wine, traveling, good conversation, and quiet times either together or alone?

Well, thanks for your time, Cupid. When the right lady reads this give her heart a little nudge.

Have her write back immediately.

Fun sized!

I'm five feet fun and a half and full of laughter and joy. How they got so much energy into little ol' me without exploding is one big mystery. When I start giggling everyone starts giggling. When I bounce into a room better hold onto your hat. The only thing bigger than my laugh is my heart.

The fella I'm looking for doesn't take himself too seriously. He's a man and treats me like a woman. We enjoy doing things together and enjoy doing things apart. There's my life, your life, and our life. Simple, not complicated.

I talk much better than I write. So if you think this profile is great wait until you meet me!

Don't make me wait too long.

I'm kind of like my dog…

…happy, playful, energetic, enthusiastic, loyal, and trusting. The similarity ends there since I don't shed, bark all night or chew up shoes.

How about you? Are you searching for a good companion? A faithful friend? A comrade to walk beside you through good times and bad?

That's me, no more, no less. But I don't sit up and beg.

Now fetch your keyboard and write me back. Good boy!

Who wants to show me around?

New here and don't have a clue. Where's a good Thai restaurant? Are there any good museums around? What about a laid-back club with great music but not so loud you can't have a conversation?

So I moved here from the sticks for my job. By sticks I mean upstate and small town. By job I mean respiratory therapist. I came here because I always wanted to live in the city. So far I love it. I mean where else can you order Chinese take-out at four in the morning?

So hit me up with the 411. We'll go from there.

Try this the next time you're blue…

It's easy, fast and guaranteed to lift your mood. Here's what you need:

2 sticks of butter
2 1/4 cups of sugar

4 large eggs
1 tablespoon vanilla
1 1/4 cups of cocoa powder
1/2 teaspoon salt
1 teaspoon baking powder
1 1/2 cups all-purpose flour
2 cups chocolate chips

Preheat your oven to 350 degrees. Grease a 9x13 inch pan. Mix the butter and sugar together in a microwave safe bowl. Now heat this in the microwave, stirring every 30 seconds, until the mixture is smooth and bubbly.

Now add in the eggs and vanilla and stir until smooth. Mix together the cocoa powder, salt, baking powder, and flour and then add to the butter mixture. Mix until smooth. Next stir in the chocolate chips. Now pour the batter into the pan. Then bake for about 28 minutes.

Yes, this is the classic brownie recipe but once you try them you'll feel absolutely great.

You'll feel the same way about me. So take off your oven mitt and write back.

Oh, you hate your job?

Why didn't you say so? There's a support group for that -- it's called EVERYBODY and they meet at the bar.

To tell you the truth I actually like my job. I work in sales at a big electronics store so I get to have fun with all the latest technology. I know my way around smartphones and computers and big screen

TVs and pretty much everything else we carry. Which is why I like coming to work since it's like a big playground to me.

Are you a gamer? If not I could show you some great ones you'd love. I own most of the classics like the Legend of Zelda, Super Mario, the Sims and so forth. They're a blast.

So what are your favorite games? I know some cool cheat codes and Easter eggs I could share. Just email and ask.

What are your favorite passport stamps?

Some countries have pretty cool passport stamps but I don't judge them by appearance. Instead, I judge them by memories.

When I think of Nepal I remember Mount Everest and a great helicopter ride. Italy brings up recollections of very fine dining. Egypt was where the camel bit me. India, well, how much time do you have?

Since I'm an independent contractor in IT I get to make my own hours. And every year I take off for two months to explore the world. Man, have I seen some things. And I've got some great stories.

I'd love to share them with you. And then maybe, if things work out, we could build some great memories together.

Let me know. It's a big world out there and the possibilities are endless.

Let me introduce you to my newest hobby...

It's called golf and I know you've heard of it. I never gave it a second thought until a buddy of mine dragged me out onto the links by promising that after 18 holes he'd buy me all the cold beer I wanted.

How could I lose?

Well, turned out I really liked the game. I'm out in the fresh air with good friends. I'm really just competing with myself. And there's nothing like an ice cold brew to celebrate the 19th hole.

If you play golf I'd love you to show me some pointers. If you don't play golf we could learn together (I'm still really terrible).

So drop me a line and let's chat. The beer's on me.

Sesquipedalian pedagogue seeks polysyllabic etymologist

First off, you should know I am afflicted with both ailurophilia and canophilia and I'd like to find someone sharing a similar condition. I am an ardent cruciverbalist and would hope you are, too. My taste in music is decidedly acroamatic.

Let me assure you that I long ago conquered my inherent logorrhea and rarely lapse back into my previous prolix propensities. I am not overly ebrious although I will cheerfully imbibe during the proper occasion. For the record I am decidedly acapnotic.

I toil within a public phrontistery illuminating the finer points of English literature to an assemblage of scatophagous young autolatrists who consider my efforts pedantic glossalalia.

If you do not think me overly phlyarologistic and entertain the merest scintilla of interest then perhaps we might attempt a friendly colloquy. I eagerly await your rejoinder.

Chicks in chairs make beautiful roll models

When people ask why I'm in a wheelchair I tell them, 'I'm not really disabled, I'm just lazy.' That either makes them smile or go away. And that's how I roll.

Since I know you're curious I'll tell you: I was in a bad car wreck when I was sixteen. Enough said.

I'm working on my law degree and will graduate in a couple years. When I start practicing law I'll represent all the underdogs out there, the people left behind or taken advantage of or who just fall between the cracks.

I won't be doing it for the money, but to help level the playing field. I'll be like David against all the Goliaths.

Want to know what I'm calling my law firm? The Wheels of Mayhem. Didn't see that coming, did you? And neither will they.

So that's my story and I'm sticking to it. What about your story?

Just please don't be like my last boyfriend. I had to dump him. He was always pushing me around and talking behind my back.

If you think you can keep up drop me a line. But watch your toes.

I'm not yelling – I'm Italian!

And even when I'm just talking I wave my hands around. I can't be understood any other way.

So now you know – I'm expressive, passionate, emotional, and ardent. You won't ever have to wonder what my opinion is, either. It's in my blood. My ancestors were artists, sculptors, centurions, and rumor has it mafiosi.

By day I'm a professor of classical languages. Go figure!

But by night you might find me singing along with Bocelli or Gobbi or Gedda as I prepare a caprese salad while slowly simmering my home-made cacciucco. Did I tell you I love to sing! And cook!

And wait until you hear what's in my wine collection!

So did you ever wonder why they call Italian a romance language? It's a secret only Italians know, but perhaps you'll let me share that secret with you. Interested? Then contact me immediamente!

There is no future in the past

I hate to say this, but too many people here haven't gotten over their ex. You know the ones I'm talking about – they try and tell you their entire sad break-up story over your first lunch with them. Been there and done that.

Look, if you're one of them I feel for you, I know how rough it can be. But give yourself time to heal. You owe it to yourself. And to everyone else here.

If you're still reading I'm glad. It means you've packed up all your old baggage and put it in storage somewhere.

You're ready to come out and play.

Well, I'm ready, too.

I'll make you a good playmate if you like the finer things in life. Like a five-star restaurant where it takes months to get a reservation. Or opening night at the latest off-Broadway play.

Winter weekends skiing the slopes. Summer weekends snorkeling off the Keys.

It's a big world out there and my adventure is only halfway begun. If you're over the past and ready for the now then let me know.

I can be ready in 15 minutes

And I'm not kidding, either. I hate staying home. I hate watching TV. I want to be out and about and doing something cool.

Here's an example.

Last year around midnight I got a call from my best friend who told me there was an unexpected room-opening on a cruise ship. The cost was peanuts! The only catch was I had to be at the dock in an hour.

So I pulled on my sweats, slipped into my flip flops and grabbed my purse. I made it with five minutes to spare. My hair was a mess, my teeth needed brushing, and I still hadn't thought of a good excuse to tell my boss.

Bought everything I needed with my trusty credit card. Ate like a queen. Danced all night. Lazed in the sun all day. But now my problem was how to explain the new tan to my boss. But hey, jobs come and go but life is a one-time gig.

So I'm ready for anything. Just give me 15 minutes. How about you? What are you ready for?

Pick one…

Hello [screen name] [avatar] [cute epithet] [prison registration number].

I read your [lonely hearts' profile] [eBay posting] [craigslist ad] [company memo] and wanted to respond.

You really [communicate well] [seem intriguing] [look foxy] [act drunk] and I decided to write because I am [interested] [bored] [kind of drunk myself].

I like how you [made me smile] [made me think] [seem easy] [have a job]. I sense you are looking for someone who is [intellectually stimulating] [good at cuddling] [an animal lover] [proficient with the alphabet].

I enjoy [warm rainbows at sunset] [soft sandy picnics in the rain] [fuzzy little puppies in a box] [reading the great philosophers]. I have [a valid driver's license] [my own place] [Netflix] [a black Harley Davidson].

If you are interested I would really like to [talk more] [live in your back yard] [borrow some money] [see your tattoos].

In the meantime I hope you have [a great day] [the winning lottery number] [good luck with your parole hearing].

Thank you for [your time] [your ex-boyfriend's credit card number] [smiling at my silly email].

If it's worth another smile, get in touch.

One Last Word

Thanks for reading! If you enjoyed this eBook or found it useful I'd be very grateful if you'd post a short review. Your support really does make a difference and I read all the reviews personally so I can get your feedback and make my books even better.

All My Best To You!

Other books by this author:

Steal This Resume: 500 job-winning Resumes and Cover Letters you can use – ready for instant download!

Available exclusively on Amazon

Find more great books here:

www.EasyReaderPress.com

www.ingramcontent.com/pod-product-compliance
Lightning Source LLC
Chambersburg PA
CBHW061754020426
42331CB00006B/1473